At Home with the Prairie Dog

THE STORY OF A KEYSTONE SPECIES

Dorothy Hinshaw Patent

Photographs by William Muñoz

Web of Life

CHILDREN'S BOOKS

WESTERN MEADOW LARK

Birds begin singing their morning songs as dawn lightens the sky. Purple, yellow and blue wildflowers decorate the grassland. A gentle breeze blows across the vast prairie.

Atop a mound of dirt, a prairie dog peeks out of a hole—the entrance to her underground home. Is it safe to come out?

BLANKET FLOWER

LOCOWEED

Cautiously, the prairie dog emerges. Standing on her hind feet on top of the burrow, she stretches her neck to the sky, looking around and sniffing the air. Sensing no danger, she signals to her three young pups, who promptly scramble out of the burrow to play.

Above ground, a mound of soil marks the "front door" to the prairie dogs' burrow. Beyond the entrance is a complicated network of connected tunnels with several rooms. Just like a house, the rooms are used for different activities, such as sleeping and grooming.

Some rooms are furnished with dry grass for comfort. There are escape holes away from the main entrance, in case predators come to visit. Best of all, the burrow is an air-conditioned home in summer and a frost-free refuge in winter.

ESCAPE HOLE

Because the burrow is such a pleasant place to be, it is a haven for many other animals besides prairie dogs. Scientists have identified roughly 150 different kinds of animals living in and around prairie dog burrows! Prairie dogs are called a *keystone species* because so many other living things depend on them to survive.

Insects and spiders live alongside the prairie dogs in their burrows.

Toads and salamanders use the moist, cool tunnels to escape the dry heat above. The burrows help these animals survive on a treeless prairie.

TIGER SALAMANDER

DUNG BEETLE

BLACK WIDOW SPIDER

PLAINS SPADEFOOT TOAD

Occupied Burrow

second escape hole

bathroom

escape hole

bedroom

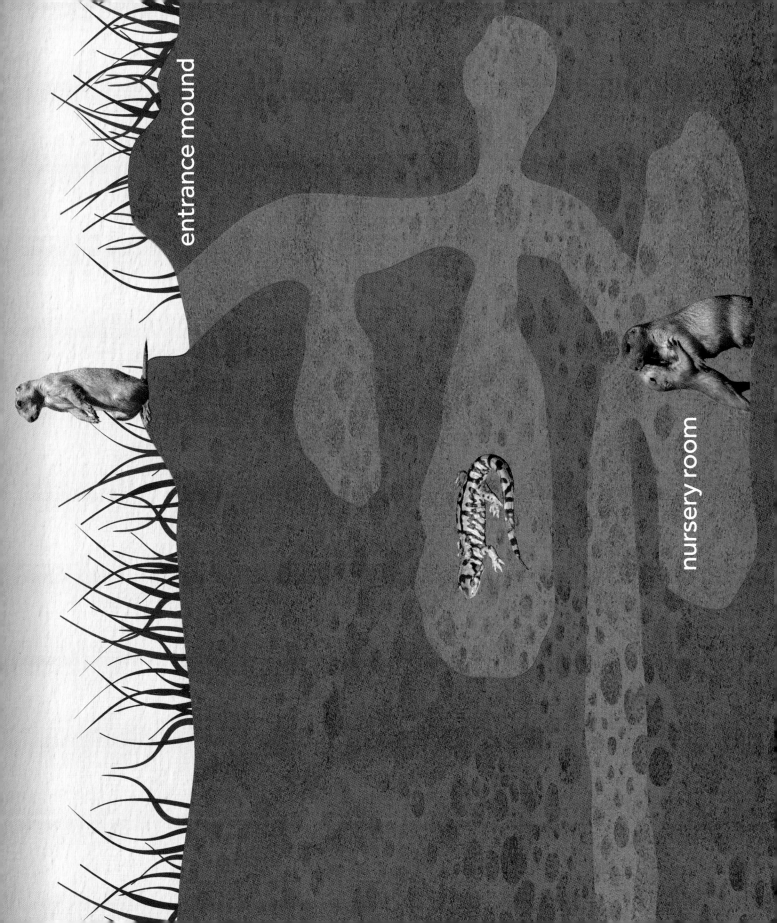

COTTONTAIL RABBIT

PRAIRIE DEER MOUSE

PRAIRIE RATTLESNAKE

BLACK-FOOTED FERRET

BURROWING OWL WITH OWLETS

Other animals seek out abandoned burrows. Burrowing owls claim them for their nests, laying their eggs and caring for their owlets until they are ready to fledge.

Deer mice and cottontails dash into abandoned burrows to evade predators.

Rattlesnakes take refuge from extreme weather in the abandoned tunnels.

Black-footed ferrets rely on abandoned burrows for shelter and raising young.

Abandoned Burrow

The pups play, explore, and nibble on wildflowers and grass. Prairie dogs are constantly clipping the grass around the burrows. Keeping the grass short makes it easier to spot predators that could be hunting nearby.

The short grass benefits other animals, too. Birds such as killdeer, horned larks, grouse and the rare mountain plover raise their families near the burrows where they can easily find and feed on insects.

GREATER SAGE-GROUSE

KILLDEER

HORNED LARK

MOUNTAIN PLOVER

BISON

MULE DEER

ELK

PRONGHORN

Large grazing animals such as pronghorn, elk, mule deer and bison also benefit from the prairie dogs' clipping.

Bison, which once roamed the prairies by the millions, prefer the short-grass "lawn" around prairie dog mounds. Grass is most nutritious when it is young and growing, and the prairie dogs' constant nibbling means there is always plenty of new growth.

The habits of prairie dogs and bison together help other prairie animals. Prairie dogs create bare areas of dirt when they dig, and bison take dust baths there. Rolling in dust helps kill parasites—like ticks—on the bisons' hide.

When it rains, the dust baths turn to mud. These mud pools, called wallows, provide drinking water for prairie residents such as pronghorn and breeding grounds for toads and salamanders.

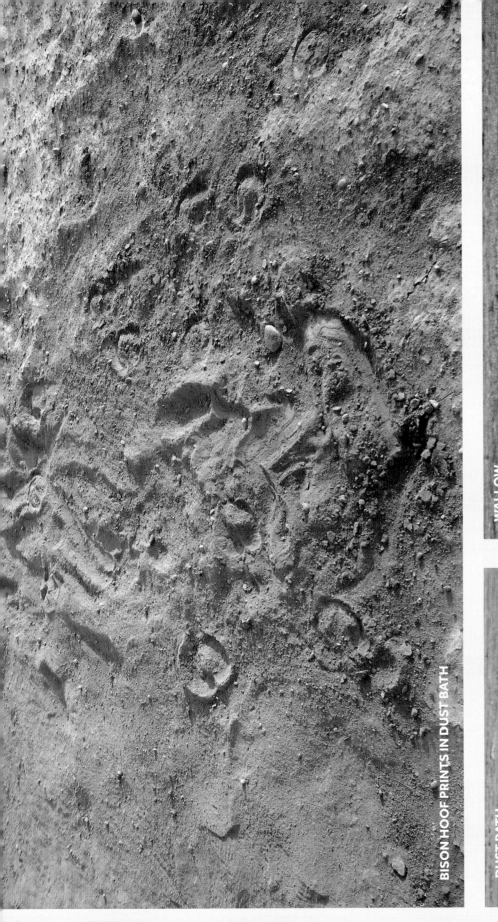

BISON HOOF PRINTS IN DUST BATH

WALLOW

DUST BATH

BLACK-FOOTED FERRET

FERRUGINOUS HAWK

SWIFT FOX

BADGER

COYOTE

Not only do the activities of prairie dogs help create a varied environment for other life, they themselves provide vital meals for many predators—hawks, coyotes, badgers, foxes and more. Highly endangered black-footed ferrets can only survive in the wild where prairie dogs are present, since prairie dogs make up 90 percent of the ferret's diet.

Prairie dogs live in large colonies called "towns," which may contain dozens of prairie dog families. Throughout the day, the mother prairie dogs keep watch between nibbles of grass or wildflowers. When they sense danger, the mothers give high-pitched warning barks, and the pups dash for their burrows. Sometimes, when they reunite, they kiss each other.

As day ends, the family retires to their cozy burrow for the night. Tomorrow will bring another day of playing, exploring and eating.

Summer soon fades into fall, and the prairie dogs eat more and more food. They will need the extra fat to help them survive the winter.

Many of the animals that benefit from the prairie dogs' work migrate in the fall. Pronghorn and bison move on to their wintering homes, well nourished after their summer grazing on the prairie.

Most of the birds that nest here in the summer fly south for the winter. They will be back next year.

Insects, toads and other small animals find winter refuge in the prairie dog burrows. They are able to survive even the coldest winter thanks to the protection the burrows provide.

The prairie dogs themselves spend most of the winter underground, only coming out now and then to peek outside. Black-footed ferrets continue to hunt prairie dogs in winter.

Come spring, a new generation of prairie dog pups will emerge to play in the carpets of wildflowers. With the help of this keystone species, the diverse prairie ecosystem will continue to thrive.

LONG-BILLED CURLEW

PRONGHORN MIGRATION

BISON

BLACK-FOOTED FERRET

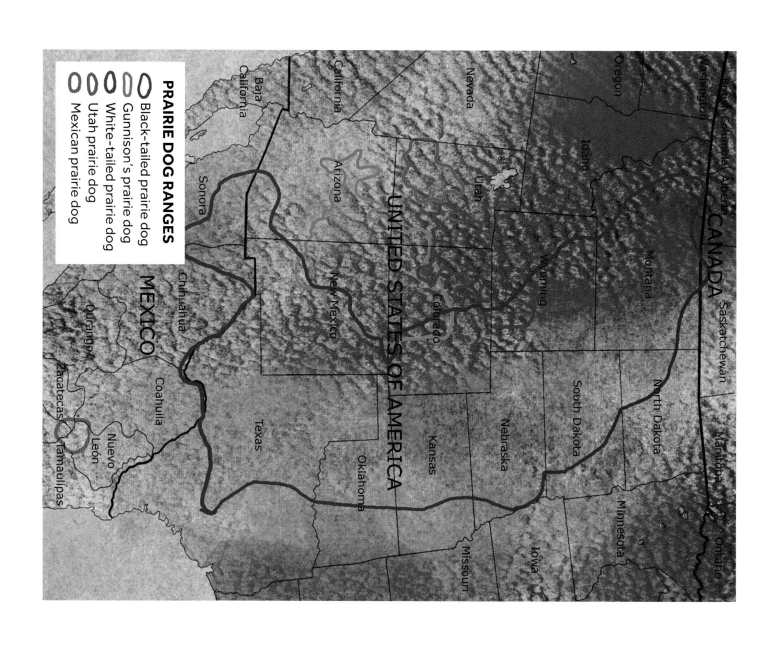

PRAIRIE DOG RANGES

- Black-tailed prairie dog
- Gunnison's prairie dog
- White-tailed prairie dog
- Utah prairie dog
- Mexican prairie dog

More About Prairie Dogs

There are five species of prairie dogs, all living in western areas of North America. The black-tailed species (scientific name *Cynomys ludovicianus*) is by far the most common and is the one represented in this book. Other species are the white-tailed prairie dog, Gunnison's prairie dog, the Mexican prairie dog, and the rare Utah prairie dog.

Highly social, black-tailed prairie dogs live in large colonies or "towns" that can span hundreds of acres. A prairie dog town may contain 15–26 family groups. Most prairie dog family groups are made up of one adult breeding male, two to three adult females and their offspring.

Their towns consist of a large number of closely spaced burrows, each with an elaborate network of tunnels and multiple entrance holes through which prairie dogs can escape predators. Prairie dog burrows are typically 5–10 m (16–33 ft) long and 2–3 m (6.6–9.8 ft) below the ground and have up to six entrances.

Black-tailed prairie dogs communicate with each other using a wide variety of sounds—from territorial calls to barely audible chirps between mothers and babies to mating calls and alarm calls.

Before non-native Americans began moving west, hundreds of millions of black-tailed prairie dogs lived in North America, from southern Saskatchewan in Canada through the middle of North America into northern Mexico. However, since the 1860s about 90 percent of the prairie dog population has been eliminated. Farms, railroads, towns, cities and ranches took over the land, leaving only scattered prairie dog towns that were diminished in size. Diseases such as the plague have also affected prairie dogs and can quickly wipe out a whole colony.

Conserving prairie dogs is important not only to preserve the animals themselves, but also to protect the many other species that depend on this keystone species. Fortunately, many organizations are working to preserve grasslands and the prairie dogs that help maintain them.

Further resources:

World Wildlife Fund
www.worldwildlife.org/places/northern-great-plains

Defenders of Wildlife
www.defenders.org/wildlife/prairie-dog

To the invaluable folks at American Prairie who are making the dream of a healthy prairie ecosystem come true.—D.H.P.

To Alice and her brothers and sisters (Jordy, Tobin, Aura and Otto).—W.M.

Special thanks to Kristy Bly, Senior Wildlife Conservation Biologist for World Wildlife Fund's Northern Great Plains Program, for generously sharing her knowledge about the lives of prairie dogs.

Text © 2023 by Dorothy Hinshaw Patent · Photographs © 2023 by William Muñoz · Graphics © 2023 by Marlo Garnsworthy

Photo acknowledgments: All of the photographs in this book were taken by William Muñoz with the exception of the following: Black-footed ferret (cover, p. 15) © NPS; burrowing owl (cover, p. 14) by Mauricio S. Ferreira, Shutterstock; plains spadefoot toad (cover, pp. 9, 10) © Adam Messer, Montana FWP; American bison (cover) by O.S. Fisher, Shutterstock; tiger salamander (cover, pp. 9, 11) by Creeping Things, Shutterstock; prairie dogs (back cover, p. 11, bottom) by Douwe, Adobe Stock; black widow spider (pp. 9, 10) by KAdams66, iStock; dung beetle (pp. 9, 10) by HWall, Shutterstock; prairie dog (p. 10, top) by Fotomaster, Adobe Stock; prairie dog (p. 10, middle) by Vladislav333222, Adobe Stock; prairie dogs (p. 10, bottom) by Mysikrysa, Adobe Stock; prairie dog (p. 11, top) by Dennis Donohue, Adobe Stock; prairie deer mouse (p. 12) © Ryan Stephans; black-footed ferret (p. 12) by Kerry Hargrove, Shutterstock; cottontail rabbit (pp. 12, 14) by Olga Mendenhall, Adobe Stock; prairie rattlesnake (p. 12) © NPS; burrowing owls (p. 13) © ClaireVisconti, NPS; burrowing owl nest (p. 14) by Rick & Nora Bowers, Alamy; deer mouse (p. 14) by Nina, Adobe Stock; burrowing owls (p. 15) by Creeping Things, Shutterstock; horned lark (p. 17) by JH Williams, iStock; greater sage-grouse (p. 17) by Danita Delimont, Adobe Stock; mountain plover (p. 17) by Agami Photo Agency, Shutterstock; killdeer (p. 17) © Sneed Collard; mule deer (p. 18) by Richard Seeley, Adobe Stock; pronghorn (p. 18) © NPS; ferruginous hawk (p. 22) by Sly, Adobe Stock; badger (p. 22) © Aaron Stiny; black-footed ferret (p. 22) by Kerry Hargrove, Shutterstock; swift fox (p. 22) by Jillian, Adobe Stock; coyote (p. 23) © Tom Koerner-USFWS; prairie dogs (p. 25, bottom) by Natalia Kuzmina, Shutterstock; prairie dogs (p. 28) © Kim Acker, NPS; long-billed curlew (p. 29) by Ken Archer/Danita Delimont, Adobe Stock; pronghorn migration (p. 29) © Dennis Jorgensen WWF-US.

For ages 5-9

Published in the United States in 2023 by Web of Life Children's Books, Berkeley, California.

Library of Congress Control Number: 2022940741 · ISBN: 978-1-970039-06-1

Book design by: Philip Krayna, Modiv Design, www.modiv.design.com

Printed in China by Toppan Leefung · Production Date: Aug of 2022 · Batch:01

For free, downloadable activities, and for more information about our books and the authors, artists and photographers who created them, visit our website: www.weboflifebooks.com

Distributed by Publishers Group West/An Ingram Brand · (800) 788-3123 · www.pgw.com

FSC
MIX
Paper from
responsible sources
FSC® C104723